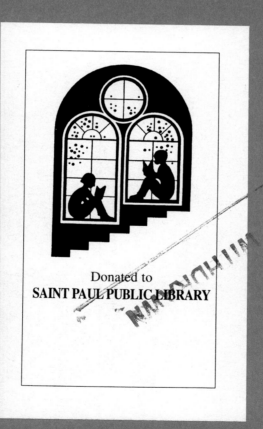

ONE GOOD APPLE

Growing Our Food for the Sake of the Earth

Catherine Paladino

HOUGHTON MIFFLIN COMPANY
BOSTON 1999

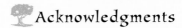

Acknowledgments

For sharing with me their wisdom and kindness, their homes, and the harvests from their fields, I wish to thank Troy, Sharon, and Indiana Bogdan; Will Bonsall, Molly Thorkildsen, and their sons, Fairfield and Kindle; John, Roberta, and Phoebe Bunker; Sue Fleming; Darrell, Linda, and Terra Frey; the Glendening family; the Johnson family; Jason, Barb, and Emma Kafka; the Kretschmann family; Denise Masayesva, Maynard Nutumya, and their family; the late Helen Nearing; Bob and Viola Omlor; and John Robinson. Also thanks to Ralph K. Bell, Cara Goldberg, Abel LaBelle, Steve Page, John Pino, Bob Sewall, and Jayne Thomisee.

For reference books, articles, and photographs, I thank Scott R. Bauer of the USDA Agricultural Research Service; Shirley A. Briggs of the Rachel Carson History Project; Elizabeth Donohoe; Thomas Featherstone of the Walter P. Reuther Library, Wayne State University; Laurie Formichella of the Beverly Public Library, Beverly, Massachusetts; Marc and Cheryl Harshman; Dorothy Hayes; Jocelyn Sherman; Richard Steven Street; and Virginia Thorburn.

My sincere thanks to Chuck Benbrook; Kate Clancy; Kevin Dahl; Jean English; Dolores Huerta; Nicolas Lindholm; Dr. Marion Moses; Angelo J. Joaquin, Jr., executive director, and the staff of Native Seeds/SEARCH; the Organic Crop Improvement Association, Western Pennsylvania Chapter; the Rodale Institute staff; Elizabeth Scott-Graham; Lauren Shorsher; and John Wargo, for sharing their expertise.

I am grateful to Luz and Maura Castro and Sharon Delores of the Indian Oasis Primary School Dancers, and to Zetta Masayesva, for allowing me to photograph them during the Native Seeds/SEARCH and Tucson Botanical Gardens Chile Fiesta; to Neil Lash, Jon Thurston, and Beth Ezell of the Medomak Valley High School Heirloom Seed Project; Fedco Seeds of Maine for letting me photograph their Common Ground Country Fair booth; Renee Mease and the children of Antietam Academy, Mt. Penn, Pennsylvania; and Seth and Josiah Brown for being on the book's cover.

I would like to thank Russell Libby, executive director of the Maine Organic Farmers and Gardeners Association, for his expert reading of this manuscript and for his encouragement from the very beginning; Kim Keller of Houghton Mifflin Company for coordinating the details; designer Chris Hammill Paul for adding her creative vision; and copy editor Peg Anderson for her gift of clarity. My deepest thanks to my editor, Ann Rider, for seeing this book through its rather long journey and for her keen discernment, as always, of what is most important.

Finally, I thank my husband, Scott Thorburn, for his help and patience, and for our children — Lukas, who has been my other set of eyes and ears, and Chloë, whose birth during this project gave it new life.

Cover photo: photographed at Sewall's Orchards, Lincolnville, Maine
Back jacket photo: photographed at Khadighar farm, Farmington, Maine

Book design by Chris Hammill Paul.   The text of this book is set in 13.5 point Horley Old Style.

Library of Congress Cataloging-in-Publication Data

Paladino, Catherine.
     One good apple : growing our food for the sake of the earth / Catherine Paladino.
          p. cm.
     Summary: Discusses the problems created by the use of pesticides to grow food crops and the benefits of organic farming.
          ISBN 0-395-85009-6
     1. Organic farming—Juvenile literature. 2. Natural foods—Juvenile literature. 3. Food crops—Juvenile literature.
     4. Pesticide residues in food—Juvenile literature. [1. Pesticides. 2. Organic farming. 3. Agriculture—
     Environmental aspects.] I. Title.
          S605.5.P35   1999
          363.738'4—dc21   97-45866 CIP AC

Printed in Singapore

TWP   10   9   8   7   6   5   4   3   2   1

This book is for Rachel Carson,
whose courageous words
may save us yet

"Can anyone believe it is possible to lay down such a barrage of poisons
on the surface of the earth without making it unfit for all life?"
—Rachel Carson, *Silent Spring*

If the Bill of Rights contains no guarantee that a citizen shall be secure against lethal poisons distributed either by private individuals or by public officials, it is surely only because our forefathers, despite their considerable wisdom and foresight, could conceive of no such problem.

—Rachel Carson, *Silent Spring*

 **REACH FOR AN APPLE** the next time you are in a grocery store and hold it in your hand. Then try to describe it. What color is it? Does it smell sweet? Is it shiny and smooth or bruised and bumpy? What variety of apple is it? Can you tell if any insects tried to eat your apple while it was growing?

Maybe you have never thought so much about an apple before. But the more you know about your apple and where it came from, the more likely you may be to think twice about eating it. If it is an especially big, bright red apple, with polished skin and no spots or worm holes, the chances are that the apple is not really as pure and wholesome as it looks. For in order to grow the large, perfect-looking fruits and vegetables so common in supermarkets these days, farmers have come to rely on poisons.

These poisons are pesticides, man-made chemicals in the form of powders, sprays, or gases, that are used to kill insects, weeds, fungi (mold), and other living things that might damage crops. Farmers also use pesticides to make fruits and vegetables look as attractive as possible. An unblemished apple sells for more money than one with a scar left by an insect bite.

Pesticides may be insecticides, herbicides (weed killers), or fungicides. They are applied to seeds, to crop plants as they are growing, and to harvested fruits and vegetables. They are also put into the soil.

Some pesticides wash off in the rain or break down into less harmful substances in sunlight. But many do not. They remain on leaves and stems and on the skins of fruits and vegetables. Certain

Apples are often coated with wax to protect them and make them look shinier. Tomatoes, nectarines, cucumbers, peppers, and other foods are sometimes waxed, too. Waxing seals in pesticide residues. Washing a waxed apple would not remove any residues that may be on its skin; only peeling it would.

pesticides used on crops such as potatoes and peanuts get absorbed by the plant's leaves or roots and spread into all of its parts, including those we eat. Although we cannot see them, very small amounts of pesticides are in or on most of the fruits and vegetables sold in every supermarket in the country. We call these invisible traces pesticide residues.

Pesticide residues in food are not a new problem. Before the 1940s, farmers used natural poisons made from minerals found in the earth's crust to control crop pests and diseases. These early pesticides included toxic compounds of sulfur, lead, mercury, copper, and arsenic. Chemical residues on produce were so heavy at times that they were even visible. In 1891, for example, an article in the *New York Times* with the headline "Poisoned Grapes on Sale" reported that a greenish powder found on grapes was the fungicide copper sulfate.

Apples often arrived at markets covered with arsenic powder during the early 1900s. In those days farmers commonly sprayed their orchards with an arsenic compound called lead arsenate to control the number-one pest of apple trees: the codling moth. Codling moth caterpillars—the "worms" in wormy apples—are big apple eaters.

At that time the toxic effects of arsenic had been known for centuries, but careless agricultural spraying still resulted in poisonings of livestock, bees, deer, fish, and humans. Hazardous though they were, pesticides often meant the difference between success and failure of a crop. Farmers were therefore reluctant to give them up. This difficult situation remains true in agriculture today — only now the chemicals have changed.

This sign on a shed in a New England apple orchard bears a grave warning about the pesticides stored inside. Despite the hazards of pesticides to all forms of life, chemical companies continue to manufacture and sell new ones to farmers every year. In 1995 nearly one billion pounds of pesticides were applied to American farmlands.

☞ This notice, published in the November 26, 1925, issue of the *New York Times*, reports that the British discovered a high level of arsenic in American apples. The British government considered this level unsafe and threatened to stop importing apples from the United States.

In 1939 a Swiss scientist named Paul Müller discovered that the man-made chemical DDT was very effective at killing insects. American military and public health officials immediately put this knowledge to use during World War II to prevent the spread of malaria among U.S. soldiers stationed in tropical areas. Sprayed from airplanes over South Pacific islands, DDT killed the mosquitoes that carried the deadly disease. In its years of use DDT probably helped to save millions of people's lives. Müller won the Nobel Prize for his discovery.

After the war ended in 1945, we found another use for DDT—controlling insect pests on farms. DDT worked so quickly and was so powerful that many farmers no longer bothered with the old pesticides. Chemical manufacturers invented more and more new pesticides to sell to farmers. Some of them were like DDT, while others resembled another wartime poison — nerve gas. Unlike the old compounds, the new pesticides had chemical structures based on carbon atoms, which are the very building blocks of life. Thus in some ways they resembled the molecules made by living cells. Yet they had never before existed in nature. How such chemicals would behave outside the laboratory and how they would affect organisms could not truly be known until after they were released into the environment.

At first, the effects of the new man-made, or synthetic, chemicals appeared miraculous. Farmers believed they could "win the battle" against insects and weeds, and the land could be made to produce more food per acre than ever before. Small farms grew larger because pesticides enabled farmers to manage more acres. The chemical industry was thriving. The modern pesticide age had begun.

But amid all the optimism, some people were beginning to suspect that pesticides might be doing more harm than good. One of those people was the biologist and author Rachel Carson. In 1962 Carson published a book called *Silent Spring*, which changed the way the world thought about pesticides. Shocking examples of how humans and wildlife were being poisoned by these chemicals filled the book. Rachel Carson predicted that our clumsy, shortsighted attempts to eradicate insects such as the Japanese beetle without regard for the balance of nature would have dire consequences for the environment and our health. She was right.

Silent Spring described how DDT and other man-made pesticides disrupted the normal chemical processes of living things that came in contact with them. They damaged the brain, liver, nerves, chromosomes, and reproductive organs, the book said, and they could cause cancer. Not until ten years after *Silent Spring* was published, though, did the United States government finally ban the use of DDT. And, although using DDT is now illegal in this country, we still export it to other countries. Leftover in the soil from years ago, this persistent chemical takes decades to break down. It continues to contaminate our spinach and root crops such as carrots and potatoes. DDT will be with us for a long time.

Rachel Carson on Hawk Mountain, Pennsylvania, 1945. Photo by Shirley A. Briggs, used by permission of Rachel Carson History Project

As a biologist for the U.S. Fish and Wildlife Service, Rachel Carson began reading disturbing scientific reports during the 1940s and 1950s of birds and fish dying in areas where DDT was sprayed to kill insects.

Silent Spring showed how the widespread spraying of DDT for pest control had wiped out whole populations of birds and had nearly caused bald eagles to go extinct.

Pound for pound, many of the pesticides used to grow our food today are far more toxic than older products like DDT; smaller amounts have the same killing effect. But pesticide use in this country has more than doubled since *Silent Spring* was published more than thirty-five years ago. Where do all of these toxic chemicals go once they have been released into the environment? The answer, quite simply, is *everywhere*.

Pesticides are found in soil, air, and water; in rain, snow, and fog. They are carried around the world by wind and ocean currents and have been detected at both poles of the earth. Nearly every one of us breathes air, drinks water, and eats food that is contaminated with pesticides. These toxic chemicals circulate in the bloodstream and end up in our organs. They have been found in newborn babies and in mothers' milk. Over the last fifty years, certain kinds of cancers, blood and nerve disorders, birth defects, and problems with reproduction have become more common, and many scientists believe that synthetic pesticides are at least partly to blame.

The Environmental Protection Agency (EPA) sets limits for the amounts of pesticides that may remain on foods when they reach the grocery store. These legal limits are called tolerances. Currently, about 325 of the chemicals used to make pesticides are allowed as residues. For every one of these chemicals a separate tolerance is set for each kind of food that it may be used on. Some of the chemicals

☞ To satisfy the demand for year-round fruits and vegetables, every year the United States imports more and more produce from tropical and semitropical countries, where pesticide use is heavy and less strictly regulated than it is here. Chemicals that we have banned but still sell abroad can come back to us as residues on imported food, a cycle known as the "circle of poison."

All kinds of wild animals, including frogs, birds, fish, turtles, and alligators—even polar bears and penguins—have been found with pesticides in their bodies. When domestic animals such as cows and chickens eat pesticide-contaminated feed, their milk and eggs become contaminated too.

are used on as many as 100 different crops, making the entire list of tolerances nearly 10,000 items long.

When the government started setting legal limits for pesticide residues in foods back in the 1950s, little was known about their health risks. The enormous list of tolerances is now outdated and must be revised, which is an overwhelming task for the EPA. To demonstrate the size of the problem, a Yale University professor of environmental studies, John Wargo, once brought a copy of the list to class to show his students. It wrapped around the entire lecture hall.

The legal limits of pesticides in foods have been set according to what is considered safe for adults. In 1988 a team of researchers working for the National Academy of Sciences set out to determine whether these levels were low enough to protect the health of children. John Wargo of Yale was on that team. Nicknamed the "Kids Committee," it studied how children's bodies and eating habits differ from adults'. In 1993 the Kids Committee published

Corn in all its forms—corn on the cob, popcorn, corn flakes, corn chips, corn bread—is a regular part of many children's diets. Corn oil and corn syrup are commonly used in processed foods such as bread and peanut butter. Grown to feed both people and livestock, corn is a major American crop on which enormous amounts of herbicides are used.

an important report called *Pesticides in the Diets of Infants and Children*. Babies and children, the report said, are at greater health risk from pesticides in food than adults are for several reasons.

First, children's organs are still forming and are more sensitive to toxic chemicals than the fully formed organs of adults. Second, since children are growing at a much faster rate, they eat more food in relation to their body size than adults do. Thus children may ingest more pesticide residues per pound of body weight than adults do. And finally, young people tend to eat a lot of a few favorite foods. Eating the same foods day after day, such as apples or peanut butter or grapes, may mean getting a higher than average dose of whatever pesticides they contain. For all of these reasons, the Kids Committee concluded that the legal limits on pesticide residues did not guarantee protection for children.

Measuring pesticide residues is like detecting a drop of food coloring in a child's wading pool full of water. It requires sensitive laboratory equipment. To keep track of the levels of chemical residues in our food supply, the United States Department of Agriculture (USDA) began regular testing of food samples in 1991.

The tests show that a single food may contain residues of several different pesticides. In 1993, for example, one apple sample contained nine different pesticides. In 1995, samples of eleven kinds of fruits and vegetables, including apples, bananas, grapes, and green beans, contained sixty-nine different pesticides. Indeed, almost two-thirds of the food samples that year had pesticide residues, usually of more than one kind.

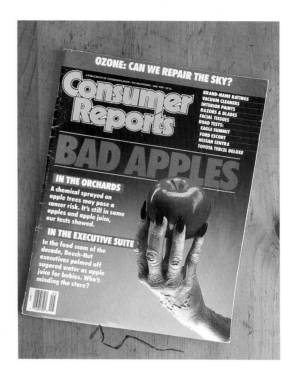

Nine of every ten apple samples in the USDA tests had residues, even after washing. Apples were the focus of a pesticide scare in the late 1980s when much of the U.S. red apple crop was being sprayed with Alar, a chemical that was found to cause cancer in laboratory animals. Alar was used to keep the apples from falling off the trees too early, make them firmer, and turn them a deep, dark red. Alarming media reports about the dangers of Alar prompted many people to stop buying apples and apple products until farmers stopped using it. The EPA finally banned the use of Alar on food crops in 1992.

The Alar scare, along with the Kids Committee report, helped convince the federal government to rewrite the laws on pesticide residues in foods. In the summer of 1996, the U.S. Congress passed the Food Quality Protection Act. This law requires the EPA to set stricter safety limits (meaning lower tolerance levels) on pesticide residues to protect infants and children.

The new limits must also take into account the fact that people are exposed not to just one chemical at a time but to *mixtures* of pesticides in food and drinking water. Scientists have discovered

During the Alar scare, headlines like this one drew public attention to the issue of pesticide residues in food. Whether or not the health risks from Alar were exaggerated, as some people now think, taking one chemical off the list of nearly a hundred that apple growers use does not mean that apples are safer today.

that the effect of a mixture of pesticides may be hundreds of times stronger than the effect of each pesticide by itself. Typical meals that we eat contain mixtures of pesticides. But since the EPA considered only the effects of each pesticide singly when setting legal limits, we cannot be sure that those levels are safe.

The EPA has been given ten years to adjust the nearly 10,000 existing pesticide tolerances, but this painstaking job will probably take even longer than that. In the meantime, whether the act will really protect consumers is not yet clear. The only sure way to lower pesticide residues in food is to reduce the amounts of chemicals we spray on it.

To get an idea of the total amounts of residues children consume each day, researchers for an environmental organization called the Environmental Working Group (EWG) did a study in 1998. They combined the USDA data on residues in foods with surveys of children's eating habits. The researchers estimated that every day 1.1 million American children under age six eat more than what the EPA considers a "safe" daily dose of pesticides. Residues added up to unsafe daily doses most often in apples, peaches, applesauce, popcorn, grapes, corn chips, and apple juice because children ate more of these foods than they did of others. About half the estimated unsafe doses were from the eating of apple products alone.

Occasionally, mistakes in the ways pesticides are used result in dangerously high residue levels that cause serious illness. In the early 1990s, a fifteen-year-old soccer player in Ireland got sick during a match. Five minutes

> Pesticide residue levels are not usually high enough to cause immediate, obvious symptoms of poisoning. But many health experts believe that the small amounts of toxic chemicals we eat with our food each day could have damaging long-term health effects.

into the game, the boy complained to his coach of having blurred vision and a strange feeling on his arms and legs that he described as a "wriggling under my skin like worms." His speech became slurred, and the coach mistakenly thought he was drunk. Sweating and twitching uncontrollably, the boy was taken to the hospital, where he developed abdominal pain and diarrhea.

What had caused the boy's sudden and mysterious symptoms? Half an hour before the soccer game he had eaten part of a cucumber and some yogurt. The culprit turned out to be the cucumber. Doctors had traced a recent outbreak of food poisoning in Dublin, Ireland, to some cucumbers contaminated with residues of a pesticide called aldicarb. Cucumbers contaminated with this pesticide have also caused food poisoning in the United States, even though using aldicarb on cucumbers is illegal. Aldicarb is an extremely toxic pesticide used to control mites, aphids, and tiny worms called nematodes. By law, U.S. farmers may use it on certain crops, including oranges, peanuts, sugar cane, and potatoes.

Aside from contaminating food, pesticides can cause harm to humans in other ways. Farmers, farm workers, pesticide appliers, and people who work in or live near pesticide factories are all at risk of inhaling the chemicals or absorbing them through their skin. On December 3, 1984, a cloud of toxic gas escaped from the Union Carbide pesticide plant in the city of Bhopal, India, killing more

In 1985, the illegal use of aldicarb on watermelons in California caused the largest known outbreak of pesticide food poisoning in North America. More than 1,000 people who ate contaminated watermelons over the Fourth of July holiday became ill, some with severe symptoms of vomiting, abnormal heartbeats, and seizures.

than 2,500 people and injuring more than 200,000. It was the worst case of industrial poisoning in history. The chemical that leaked is used to make aldicarb.

Every day the people who plant and harvest crops on farms that use pesticides risk being poisoned. Most of the fresh fruit and vegetable crops grown in America are cultivated or picked by hand by migrant farm workers on huge farms in California, Florida, Texas, and the Midwest. Migrant workers generally do not have other ways to earn a living; they often endure dangerous working conditions for fear of losing their jobs.

After a field is sprayed with pesticides, farm workers are not supposed to enter it before the spray has dried or the dust has settled. With highly toxic pesticides a longer waiting period, several days or more, is necessary to protect workers from contamination. But workers sometimes go into fields that are still wet with pesticides, unknowingly risking illness or death because they haven't been warned of the danger.

Pesticides sprayed on fields from airplanes or helicopters often drift in the wind onto neighboring fields. In fact, more than half of the pesticide sprayed may miss its target because of wind. Because spray drift is common in the fields of California, farm workers occasionally get hit with a shower of pesticides while working.

Children of farm workers face the same risk of exposure to pesticides in the fields as their parents do, since many of them accompany their mothers and fathers to work. Pesticides also drift into the camps where

Crop-dusting planes spray pesticides over vast fields in California, where more than half of our nation's produce is grown. They fly over so frequently that one former California farm worker likened working in the fields to being in a war zone.

Photo by Richard Steven Street

Photo by Richard Steven Street

 Looking like an astronaut, a pesticide applier sprays peach trees with fungicide. The protective gear is uncomfortable and hard to work in under the hot California sun, so farm workers often go without it.

migrant families live, exposing children at home, too. Even before birth, children whose parents apply pesticides are at risk. Researchers found that in the major crop-growing regions of Minnesota, babies whose fathers worked as pesticide appliers had more birth defects than other babies.

The rate of cancer among children is higher in some agricultural communities than in nonagricultural communities. In McFarland, California, the number of children with cancer is three times the national average. McFarland is in Kern County, which uses more pesticides than almost all other counties in the state.

Dr. Marion Moses is a physician who has cared for many farm workers poisoned by pesticides. To help educate workers and the public about the hazards of these chemicals, she started the Pesticide Education Center in California in 1988. Dr. Moses believes that if the fields are made safer for farm workers, the food they harvest will be safer for everyone. "If you protect the farm worker in the workplace, I guarantee you will protect the consumer in the marketplace," she says.

Grapes have long been one of the most heavily sprayed fresh

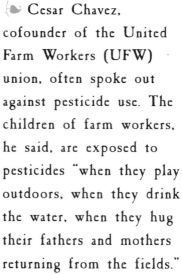

🐦 Cesar Chavez, cofounder of the United Farm Workers (UFW) union, often spoke out against pesticide use. The children of farm workers, he said, are exposed to pesticides "when they play outdoors, when they drink the water, when they hug their fathers and mothers returning from the fields."

🐦 During the 1980s, people across the country joined the UFW grape boycott, urging Americans not to buy "poisoned" grapes. According to UFW cofounder Dolores Huerta, the boycott persuaded grape growers to stop using several of the most dangerous pesticides on their fields.

food crops. Now strawberries are, too. Some strawberry growers use as much as 500 pounds of pesticides per acre on their fields. Many of the chemicals are fungicides that keep the berries from getting moldy. Strawberry workers sometimes develop raw, sore rashes on their hands from picking berries with pesticides on them.

In 1995 strawberries ranked first in a list of the twelve most contaminated fruits and vegetables, which also included grapes, apples, peaches, and cherries. In other words, strawberries had the highest levels of residues of the most toxic pesticides, according to research done by the Environmental Working Group. These pesticides include cancer-causing chemicals, nerve poisons, and chemicals that mimic our hormones and interfere with their biological signals. Hormones are natural chemicals made by our cells that enable us to grow and reproduce normally.

Photo by Jocelyn Sherman. Courtesy of Archives of Labor and Urban Affairs, Wayne State University

Photo courtesy of Archives of Labor and Urban Affairs, Wayne State University

To grow the huge red berries that have become so familiar in the supermarket, strawberry growers in California try to sterilize the soil before they even put the plants in the ground. Tractors move along the vast fields injecting a deadly gas called methyl bromide into the earth. The gas fills every earthworm tunnel, every mole burrow, every crack in the soil—and kills everything it touches. This treatment is called fumigation. Afterward, with little to get in their way, the strawberry plants grow big roots and lots of big strawberries.

At five dollars a tray, these beautiful-looking California strawberries at a Pittsburgh market may seem like a bargain. But the real cost includes damage to the environment from pesticides, health risks to farm workers, and pollution caused by trucking them across the country. Many people believe that if the price of our produce reflected those costs, farming with pesticides would no longer be economical.

Walnut Acres farm in central Pennsylvania has been organic since it started in 1946, when American agriculture was entering its chemical age. DDT had just been released for civilian use the year before. Because highway departments routinely spray herbicides along roadsides to clear them of weeds, the farm posts signs instructing sprayers to stay away from its fields.

Though sheets of plastic seal the methyl bromide into the soil, sometimes the gas leaks out and drifts into nearby communities, engulfing buildings and forcing people to evacuate their homes and schools. Because methyl bromide also destroys the earth's protective ozone layer, the federal Clean Air Act requires that we stop producing it by the year 2001. Use of methyl bromide could continue, however, as long as stockpiles of this deadly chemical last. New pesticides are already being developed to replace it, but most of them are no better, and some could even be worse.

Not all farmers use synthetic pesticides. Those who don't are called organic farmers. Organic farming is our best hope for growing food in a way that does not harm the earth or ourselves. To Don Kretschmann, an organic farmer in western Pennsylvania, farming organically means "encouraging life in the soil." "I like to define it as bringing the earth to life," he says.

The organically grown strawberries that Don Kretschmann and his daughter Grace are picking look tiny compared to the plum-sized berries from California. But they taste more like the flavorful berries our grandparents ate, and the farm's local customers look forward to the couple of weeks in June when the strawberries are ripe.

At first glance, you might overlook the small strawberry patch tucked into a slope between the apple orchard and the potato field at Kretschmann Farm. Weeds like purple thistles and quackgrass grow up around the strawberry plants. Though they seem to have taken over, the weeds actually provide shelter for fireflies that eat the slugs that like to eat the strawberries.

Customers can subscribe to Kretschmann Farm and receive a crate full of organically grown fruits and vegetables every week of the growing season. This arrangement between a farm and local families is called Community Supported Agriculture. CSAs, as such farms are called, are becoming popular all over the country. They give people a way to buy fresh organic produce that is grown close to home and a way to get to know their farmer. In turn, CSAs provide small farmers with a guaranteed customer base.

Buying food from a local farm instead of from a distant agribusiness — a large-scale farm run by a corporation — has many benefits. First, it cuts down on the fuel used for shipping and thus causes less pollution. Second, some nutrients in fruits and vegetables break down during shipping and storage, so the sooner produce is eaten after harvesting, the better. And third, fruits and vegetables

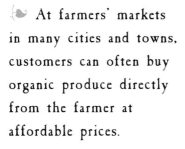

At farmers' markets in many cities and towns, customers can often buy organic produce directly from the farmer at affordable prices.

that have spent less time traveling and more time ripening in the fields taste better.

Tomatoes, for example, need to ripen on the vine to reach full flavor and vitamin C content. But a lot of supermarket tomatoes seem hard and flavorless, like baseballs. Packed and shipped while still green, they are then treated with gas to make them ripen while in storage. Tomatoes like these are grown for the traits that make them travel better without squishing and sit on a shelf longer without rotting, not for good flavor or high nutritional value.

👉 The tomatoes in this collection, grown and gathered by Roberta Bunker of Maine, each have different traits. Some of them taste sweet, for example, while others are spicy; some are juicy and others more dry. Keeping different varieties of each crop is like having a treasure chest of traits to choose from. Whenever weather, soil, or pest conditions cause one variety to fail, a different one may thrive.

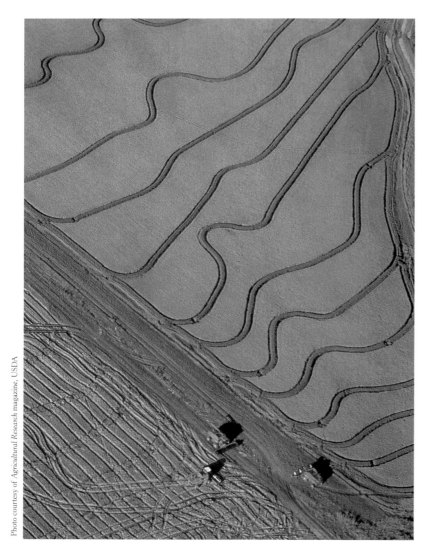

More and more, large seed companies breed crop plants that are suited for mechanized, factorylike farming—crops that can be planted and harvested by machines. Together with pesticides, modern farm machinery made possible the gradual switch in agriculture from small farms that grew many kinds of crops to huge farms that grow just one or a few. A large tract of land planted in nothing but wheat or corn or some other single crop is called a monoculture.

Monocultures are vulnerable to attack from insects and disease. When insects find row upon row of their favorite food, they will settle in to eat and reproduce on a grand scale. Monocultures, therefore, require the heavy use of pesticides. Not surprisingly, some of the chemical companies that make pesticides are also in the seed

This aerial view of rice harvesting in Texas shows how monocultures dramatically alter the landscape. According to the USDA, in 1993 a single rice variety covered 600,000 acres in Arkansas, Louisiana, Mississippi, and Texas.

business, designing crops on which their pesticides will be used.

Throughout history, gardeners and farmers have saved seeds from plants with the most desirable traits to grow the following year. Families passed seeds down from one generation to the next; neighbors swapped them. In this way, hundreds of different varieties of tomatoes, corn, beans, and other crops, each suited to its own locality, were gradually developed. Today, however, only a few varieties of each fruit, vegetable, and grain are commercially available. For example, more than 2,000 potato varieties exist in the world, but only four types make up three-quarters of the U.S. potato crop.

NEVER AGAIN SHOULD A PEOPLE STARVE IN A WORLD OF PLENTY

This statue in Cambridge, Massachusetts, commemorates the victims of the Irish potato famine of 1845–1850. The famine was a prime example of the disastrous results of lack of diversity in the food supply. Potatoes were the Irish peasants' main food then, and farmers planted mostly one common variety. When a fungal disease called late blight caused potatoes to rot in the fields, nearly a million people starved or died from diseases. Only by planting a blight-resistant variety could the farmers restore the potato crop. Even with the use of fungicides, blights still damage potatoes and other crops. More recent blight outbreaks in this country—a corn blight in 1970 and a wheat blight in the 1990s—also caused huge crop losses, illustrating the danger of planting only a few varieties of important crops.

Some organic farmers and gardeners like to grow old-fashioned, or heirloom, varieties of fruits and vegetables for their rich flavors and other special traits that modern crops do not have. Raising heirloom varieties is one way that organic farmers help preserve biodiversity, that is, the variety of traits in living things. In food crops, these traits include color, flavor, shape, size, texture, ripening time, and nutritional value. Many heirlooms have such valuable

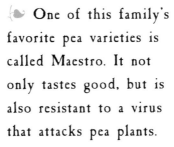

One of this family's favorite pea varieties is called Maestro. It not only tastes good, but is also resistant to a virus that attacks pea plants.

Because Fairfield Bonsall's family is so busy harvesting crops before the first frost, they grow a sauce tomato that ripens late for canning when they have more time. Called Royal Chico, it is no longer available from most seed companies, since people usually prefer early-ripening tomatoes. So the family saves tomato seeds for next year's crop.

traits as the ability to fight off certain diseases or insects or to survive drought, because they were developed before the time of modern chemicals and irrigation techniques. Indeed, this diversity in our food supply is essential if we are to guard against pests and disease without using chemicals.

To preserve the older crop varieties that we still have left, organizations like Native Seeds/SEARCH in Arizona and the Seed Savers Exchange in Iowa collect rare seeds from all over the world. They rely on small farmers and gardeners to continue growing the nearly forgotten varieties that might otherwise be lost, including

With her family, Zetta Masayesva grew these beautiful varieties of Hopi corn on their farm in Arizona. Planted in desert sand, Hopi corn thrives with little water. Each color is a different variety and is suited for a different purpose, such as parching; making flour, hominy, or dye; or for use in traditional ceremonies. To the Hopi people, all of their corn is sacred.

ancient Native American crops. Nicolas Lindholm started the Maine Seed Savers Network to keep such seeds in the hands of individuals rather than in the hands of commercial seed companies. "Seeds start and end the life cycle of agricultural crops," he says. "Seeds control the food chain."

Sir Albert Howard, sometimes called the founder of the modern organic farming movement, wrote that in nature "there is never any attempt at monoculture: mixed crops and mixed farming are the rule." To help prevent pest infestations, organic farmers may plant several types of crops in the same field or row. Intermingling different crops limits the supply of a pest insect's favorite food in any one place and may make the food harder for the insect to find. Thus this practice helps keep pest populations from exploding out of control.

Man-made pesticides did control insect infestations when the chemicals were first introduced in the 1940s. But farmers soon found that after spraying insecticides, not all of the pest insects died. Some of them just got up and walked away unharmed—they were resistant to the poison. As insects become resistant to more and more pesticides each year, farmers rely on new kinds and larger amounts of chemicals to control them. This unending vicious cycle of pests and pesticides has been called the "pesticide treadmill."

Codling moths have become resistant to each pesticide that apple growers have used against them, from lead arsenate in the early 1900s to DDT and parathion in the middle of the century, and now to a chemical called Guthion, which is one of the most toxic pesticides on the market today.

Farming with the use of synthetic pesticides is known as conventional farming. Most food in this country is grown conventionally. But if the label on a food says "certified organic," it means that the food was grown without the use of synthetic pesticides. Conventional farms far outnumber organic farms in this country;

🍂 Certain crops make good neighbors; when planted together, they benefit each other. Some of the first practitioners of companion planting, as we now call this technique, were Native American farmers who planted corn, beans, and squash together. In this grouping the corn stalk provides a trellis for the bean vines to climb, while the broad squash leaves below shade out weeds and keep the ground moist. Corn plants take a lot of nitrogen from the soil, which the bean plants replace. The Iroquois called these crops the "Three Sisters."

🍂 Today more than 500 insect pests are resistant to one or more pesticides. One—the green peach aphid shown here—has even been named a champion by the University of Florida's *Book of Insect Records* for being resistant to the largest number of pesticides.

only two-tenths of one percent of all farms in the United States were organic in 1994. But the situation is gradually changing. Concerned about the hazards of pesticides, one farmer after another is making the transition to farming without them. Some of today's organic farmers grew up on farms that used chemicals.

John Robinson is an organic farmer in Maine whose father grew crops using some pesticides. When he was growing up, Robinson remembers sneezing every time he walked by a caged-off area in his cellar where his father kept the DDT. Reading a copy of *Organic Farming and Gardening* magazine as a teenager made Robinson aware of another way of farming, a way that made more sense to him than using toxic chemicals.

An organic farm can be a habitat for wildlife such as toads, frogs, turtles, snakes, spiders, and birds, all of which help the farmer by eating pest insects. Stone walls provide good hiding places for toads, which may eat as many as 10,000 insects in three months.

🐦 Insect-eating birds like these purple martins help control pests on an organic farm. Dried gourds (painted white here), an idea borrowed from Native American farmers, make good birdhouses near gardens.

🐦 Lots of shamrock spiders inhabit the gardens at Three Sisters Farm in western Pennsylvania. This one has snared a Japanese beetle, a pest that has defied human efforts to eradicate it.

To farmers like John Robinson, growing food organically means more than just not using pesticides. It also means nurturing and protecting the soil. Organic farmers believe healthy soil produces healthy plants that are less bothered by pests. Rather than trying to control the natural world, as conventional farmers do, organic farmers observe and imitate the way nature works. An organic farm functions like an ecosystem: plants and animals interact with each other and their environment in ways that keep the system in balance.

By not planting the same crop in the same place every year, organic farmers can keep pest insects and diseases from gaining a foothold. Those pests that spend the winter in the soil where their favorite food was planted will emerge in spring to find something

Meredith Glendening of Longview Farm in western Pennsylvania harvests Brussels sprouts from a field where Sudan grass grew the year before. The tall, fast-growing grass was planted as a "cover crop" to protect the soil from erosion and to control weeds.

else planted in its place. The Colorado potato beetle is one pest that winters in the ground, so potatoes should be planted in different places from year to year. Crop rotation, as this practice is called, not only confounds pests, it helps keep the soil from getting worn out. Different plants take different nutrients from soil, so rotating crops ensures that a particular nutrient doesn't get used up.

Organic farmers actually encourage certain insects like ladybugs, lacewings, hover flies, robber flies, and wasps to live on their farms by providing them with food and shelter. These beneficial insects are either predators that eat pest insects or parasites that lay their eggs in them. The pest then becomes food for the parasite's larvae, or young. Predators and parasites eat aphids, caterpillars, beetle grubs, and other pests that damage food crops. Spraying fields and orchards with insecticides kills beneficial insects and pests alike. Pest insects, many of which multiply faster than predators, can move back into a field in even greater numbers than before it was sprayed if predators are not around to keep them in check.

Ladybugs and their young are voracious aphid eaters. Ladybug larvae have been known to eat as many as forty aphids per hour. Ladybugs also prey on mealybugs, scale insects, spider mites, and corn earworms. The adults supplement their diet with pollen from flowers like this yellow tansy.

Beneficial insects include the pollinators: bumblebees, honeybees, butterflies, beetles, flies, and moths. Without them, many crops would not produce fruit, and we would have no apples, pumpkins, berries, or potatoes. The loss of pollinators because of insecticide spraying is evident worldwide.

Where weeds are not wanted, organic growers cover the ground with a layer of mulch instead of weed killers. The straw mulch under these cabbages grown by Roberta Bunker of Maine keeps weeds down and holds moisture in the soil. As the straw decomposes it nourishes the crop.

Letting some areas of a farm grow wild and weedy provides habitat for beneficial insects. Weeds also help prevent soil erosion, and some are valuable soil improvers. Weed roots often grow thick and reach deep into the soil, opening up tunnels for the more delicate roots of food crops. They bring to the surface nutrients like phosphorus, potassium, and nitrogen, storing them in their stems and leaves. When hoed back into the earth, weeds decay and provide a natural fertilizer.

Terra Frey of Three Sisters Farm tries a bit of wood sorrel, which might be considered an undesirable weed by some farmers or gardeners. Edible weeds such as sorrel and chickweed surround the head of radicchio planted here. The weeds add flavor and vitamins and minerals to the mixed salad greens that are the farm's specialty.

Flowers and herbs such as the cosmos, borage, sunflowers, and poppies in this garden attract beneficial insects that feed on nectar and pollen as adults. Alyssum, coneflower, dill, yarrow, daisies, catnip, thyme, and tansy are also good lures. Weeds and wildflowers such as goldenrod and Queen Anne's lace work well too.

In a compost heap, soil organisms like earthworms, roly-poly bugs, millipedes, fungi, and bacteria break down animal and plant matter into an excellent plant food loaded with nutrients. The compost's spongy texture holds moisture and allows air to circulate through the soil. Pesticides destroy the community of organisms necessary for making such healthy, living soil.

Organic farmers replenish the nutrients in a field by growing a "green manure" crop such as winter rye or soybeans that will be tilled back into the soil. Nodules on the soybean roots contain bacteria that capture nitrogen from the air and change it into a form plants can use.

Recycling plant debris is a good way to return nutrients to the soil. Some organic farmers learned this practice from their grandparents, who grew up before most modern agricultural chemicals were invented. John Pino, an organic farmer in Maine, says his grandmother was an organic gardener and didn't even know it. He recalls the job she gave him when he was a boy. Every day Pino would bury the vegetable peelings from his grandmother's kitchen out in her garden. Over time, and with the help of earthworms and micro-organisms, this buried treasure turned into rich black soil.

Photographed at the Rodale Institute, Kutztown, Pennsylvania

Every organic farmer or gardener has a recipe for making compost. Some layer it like a cake, alternating vegetable scraps and weeds with animal manure. Others use just plain manure from cows, horses, or chickens; or just plant material such as hay, grass clippings, leaves, and wood chips. The middle of a compost pile feels warm to the touch because the materials "cook" as they decay.

In the forest this process happens naturally. Fallen leaves, twigs, and other plant and animal remains decay into a rich, dark, fluffy layer of earth called humus. Mixed with the soil, humus nourishes new life. By making humus, or compost, ourselves, we become part of this life cycle. Composting helps return nutrients to the soil that we take out when we grow and harvest our food.

Many conventional farmers believe that using compost is impractical on their large farms. Instead, they use man-made chemical fertilizers to supply the nutrients crops need to grow. Eventually, fields that have received only chemical fertilizers lose the nutrients and spongy texture provided by organic, living matter. Some people believe that foods grown in soil enriched with compost contain more nutrients than foods grown with chemical fertilizer. So far this theory has not been proven. But comparisons of foods kept in storage show that organically grown foods do not spoil as quickly as those grown with chemical fertilizers.

✒ Organic farmer Jason Kafka of Maine checks the "bulbies" on the tops of his garlic plants. Garlic planted in gardens and around fruit trees has been known to repel pest insects; garlic cloves in stored grain may keep out grain weevils; and sprays made from garlic have been used with success against both pest insects and fungal diseases. The compound in garlic that gives it its odor and effectiveness is allicin, which the plant makes with the help of soil microbes. Because the microbes require humus-rich soil, organically grown garlic is believed to be the most effective.

Like pesticides, industrially produced nitrogen fertilizers seemed to be miracle chemicals when they became widely available in the early 1900s. They made crops grow dramatically larger and produce more food per acre. But, as with pesticides, farmers needed to use more and more fertilizer every year to get the same results.

Jayne Thomisee is learning organic farming as an apprentice at Khadighar farm in Maine. She helps turn over compost made entirely of plant material by moving it from one bin to the next. Turning and mixing compost helps it break down faster so it can then be tilled into the soil.

Runoff from the conventionally farmed cornfield located nearby may contain excess nutrients that could be responsible for the abundance of water plants in this creek.

Soil that has lost its sponginess and become compacted erodes more easily. Rain or irrigation water can wash it away, along with the chemical fertilizer. This runoff contaminates waterways with excess nutrients, especially nitrogen and phosphorus, which make algae and cattails grow faster than they normally would. Floating mats of algae cut off sunlight to underwater plants that provide food and shelter for birds, fish, crabs, clams, and other wildlife. Decaying algae also uses up oxygen in the water, causing other species to suffocate. Agricultural runoff is choking some of the country's most wildlife-rich waterways, including Chesapeake Bay, the Florida Everglades, and historic French Creek in Pennsylvania.

Contaminated runoff from farmland is the biggest source of water pollution in the country. Along with fertilizers, pesticides also flow into our streams, rivers, and underground wells. Weed killers have been found in the drinking water of cities and towns from coast to coast. In midwestern communities, where farmers use a lot of weed killers in their cornfields, tests of drinking water commonly detect mixtures of several herbicides. In 1997 the Environmental Working Group found traces of ten different herbicides in a single glass of tap water in Williamsburg, Ohio, a suburb of Cincinnati.

Certainly no one intended for pesticides to end up in our drinking water. But the unintended outcomes of pesticide use have been countless and tragic. Directly or indirectly, visibly or invisibly, pesticides by definition destroy living things, from microorganisms to mammals.

Birds have always suffered greatly from pesticides that were intended for insects. Back in the 1950s and 1960s, DDT spraying caused drastic declines in the populations of birds of prey like the peregrine falcon, bald eagle, brown pelican, and osprey. Scientists learned that DDT built up in the birds' body fat when they ate other birds and fish that had eaten contaminated insects and plankton. The DDT caused the raptors' eggshells to be so thin that they broke before hatching.

All around Hawk Mountain Sanctuary in central Pennsylvania, which was a favorite spot of Rachel Carson's for bird watching, cornfields like this one cover the hillsides. In the past few years, pet dogs and cats in the area have been dying of cancers that some residents believe are linked to pesticide use on nearby farms. Runoff from the sloping cornfields could be contaminating ponds and brooks that the animals drink from, causing, some suspect, their mysterious and deadly tumors.

Hawks are particularly sensitive to toxic chemicals. Putting up hawk boxes for the birds to nest in has helped bring back hawks like this American kestrel, whose numbers have been declining because of pesticide use and habitat destruction. On farms, hawks help control grasshoppers as well as mice, which chew the bark of apple trees and eat other crops.

Major bird kills, like those Rachel Carson wrote about, are still happening today. For instance, biologists in recent years were puzzled by the return of fewer and fewer Swainson's hawks to western North America each summer. In January of 1996 they made a shocking discovery. Four thousand of the large raptors lay dead in the agricultural fields of Argentina, their winter home. They had been poisoned by pesticides used to control grasshoppers in alfalfa and sunflower fields. Ironically, the birds had been helping to keep these pests under control naturally. During their stay in South America, Swainson's hawks eat almost nothing but grasshoppers. The incident was the largest hawk kill on record.

Expecting to solve pest problems by exterminating insects has been a flawed notion from the start because insects are so adaptable. "Almost any way you find to kill an insect, it will find a way not to be killed," wrote entomologist Dr. George Georghiou of the

University of California in 1996. Expecting fruits and vegetables to be free of insects and insect damage is also unrealistic.

Nowhere is this more true, perhaps, than in an apple orchard. Steve Page runs Bear Well Orchard, a small organic orchard in Maine. Nothing rivals apples for the number of pests and diseases that affect them, he says. "I don't know anything more difficult to grow organically." Other apple growers agree. But conventional apple growers with large orchards can succeed financially only if more than ninety percent of their apples are "perfect," without blemishes, spots, or worm holes. To achieve that goal, they start spraying insecticides when codling moths infest only one of every hundred apples.

At Bear Well Orchard, the expectations are quite different.

⬝ Identifying insects and learning about their life cycles and food needs helps us understand the role each one plays in a farm ecosystem. If we don't view them as enemies, pests can teach us a lot about how to improve the way we grow our food.

"Unlike conventional orchards," Page says, "we don't expect perfect crops." He doesn't use synthetic pesticides. Instead, dragonflies, ground beetles, and tiny parasitic wasps protect the apples from codling moths and other pests. Red wooden croquet balls painted with sticky glue hang in the tree branches to catch apple maggot flies that mistake the balls for apples. Mulches help the trees grow strong roots and healthy fruit.

APPLE VARIETIES OF MAINE

TYDEMAN'S RED | VIKING | WAGNER | WASHINGTON CT | WEALTHY | WESTFIELD SEEK-NO-FURTHER | WILLIAM'S FAVORITE | WILLIAM'S PRIDE | WINE KISSED | WINTER BANANA | WINTER BLUSH | WINTHROP GREENING | WOLF RIVER | WOLF RIVER

SMOKEHOUSE | SOMERSET MAINE | SPARTAN | ENFIELD | SUMMER SWEETING | STARKY | STERN | STURMER PIPPIN | SWEET 16 | SWIFT | TOLMAN SWEET | TOMPKINS KING | TUMANGA | TWENTY OUNCE

NUTTING | OPALESCENT | PARKARED | POUND SWEET | PRIMA | RED ASTRICHAN | RED DELICIOUS | RED FIELD | RED FREE | RHODE ISLAND GRN | ROME | ST. LAWRENCE | SCOTT'S WINTER | SIR PRIZE

JORDAN RUSSET | KAVANAGH | LIBERTY | LONGFIELD | LYMAN'S EARLY SUMMER | MACOUN | McINTOSH | MILTON | MINJON | MOLLIE'S DELICIOUS | MUTSU | NODHEAD | NORSON | NORTHERN SPY

GRANNY SMITH | GRAVENSTEIN | GREEN SWEET | HAAS | HARALSON | HAZEN | HENRY LUCE | HIBERNAL | HIGH TOP SWEETING | HUDSON'S GOLDEN GEM | HYDE KING | IDARED | JONAGOLD | JONATHAN

COLE'S QUINCE | CORTLAND | COX ORANGE PIPPIN | DUCHESS | EARLY MAC | EMPIRE | FALL RED | FAMEUSE CK | FIRESIDE | FREEDOM | GALA | GINGER GOLD | GOLDEN DELICIOUS | GOLDEN RUSSET

🍎 Unlike conventional farming, which emphasizes uniformity and perfection, organic farming promotes diversity while allowing for imperfection. These apples are living proof of the great variety we once had in our food and could have again with more sustainable farming practices. They were gathered by John Bunker of Maine from abandoned orchards and backyard trees planted long ago.

"We keep a very tidy orchard," says Page, who diligently removes any fallen apples, leaf litter, loose bark, and broken branches that pests may be hiding in. And instead of relying on fungicides, Page grows apple varieties that are resistant to fungal diseases. As a result of all of these efforts, half of the orchard's harvested apples are considered "perfect" for eating. The rest are good enough for making cider, dried apples, and sauce.

In the early days of pesticide use, people believed that pesticides did more good than harm. Because food production increased so dramatically with the advent of chemical pesticides and fertilizers, the solution to world hunger seemed at hand. But the world seems to have outgrown this costly solution; hunger and malnutrition are still with us.

Now more people believe, as Rachel Carson did, that pesticides are doing more harm than good. Modern agricultural practices are not sustainable; that is, they cannot continue indefinitely because they are using up the earth's resources of soil and water and are making us sick. With the human population still growing and the amount of farmland shrinking, the time has come for a kind of agriculture that will last.

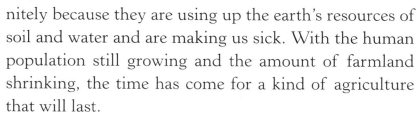

Comparisons have shown that organic farming can produce as much food per acre as conventional farming, though usually it is done on a smaller scale. Smaller local farms practicing sustainable agriculture could provide food to people living almost everywhere in the world. This approach may be a better long-term solution to hunger. Combining new knowledge with the methods of our ancestors—like crop rotation, natural pest control, and composting—today's organic farmers are growing food in a way that nourishes not only us but the earth as well.

What you can do to help grow good food for the sake of the earth:

🕊 Find out how to become an apprentice on an organic farm. Contact

> Maine Organic Farmers and Gardeners Association
> Apprentice Placement Service
> P.O. Box 2176
> Augusta, ME 04338
> (207) 622-3118

🕊 Ask your family to join a local CSA farm or go visit one. Some CSAs welcome children who want to do volunteer work. To find a CSA near you call (800) 516-7797.

🕊 Make a compost pile at home or school, even if it is just a pile of leaves. Remember, everything rots eventually. Use kitchen scraps and yard or garden wastes but no meat or dairy products. For help getting started, contact

> Rodale Institute Research Center
> 611 Siegfriedale Road
> Kutztown, PA 19530
> (610) 683-1400

🕊 Order a box of ladybugs from a beneficial insect supplier and follow the instructions for releasing them in a garden or greenhouse. Use a magnifying glass to watch them eat. Request a catalog from

> Peaceful Valley Farm Supply
> P.O. Box 2209
> Grass Valley, CA 95945
> (916) 272-4769

🕊 Grow a patch of weeds and wildflowers to attract beneficial insects. You can order the seeds from Peaceful Valley Farm Supply, listed above. Ask for the "Good Bug Blend."

🕊 Go to a farmers' market and buy your produce from the farmers who don't use pesticides. Offer to make signs for their stands or flyers that say "organically grown" to hand out to customers.

🕊 Ask the produce manager at your supermarket or food co-op to carry organic fruits and vegetables, preferably from local farms. Ask your local bakery to use flours made with organically grown grains.

🕊 Grow your own organic food in a garden at home or school. If you have only a small space, you can grow herbs in a window box, tomatoes in pots, or even potatoes in a barrel. To order heirloom and organic seeds, contact

> Native Seeds/SEARCH   Fedco Seeds
> 526 N. 4th Avenue   P.O. Box 520
> Tucson, AZ 85705   Waterville, ME 04903-0520
> (520) 622-5561
>
> Seed Savers Exchange   Turtle Tree Seed Farm
> 3076 North Winn Road   5569 N. County Road 29
> Decorah, IA 52101   Loveland, CO 80538
> (319) 382-5872

🕊 Become a member of the organic farming organization in your area (you don't have to be a farmer to join). For information, contact

> Organic Trade Association
> P.O. Box 1078
> Greenfield, MA 01302
> (413) 774-7511

🕊 Learn more about pesticides and how to avoid them. You can request newsletters and fact sheets from

> Pesticide Action Network (PAN)
> North American Regional Center
> 49 Powell Street, Suite 500
> San Francisco, CA 94102
> (415) 981-1771
> www.panna.org/panna

🕊 Grow organic bird seed—plant some sunflowers.

 Sources

The following books and articles were consulted in the preparation of this book:

Ableman, Michael. *From the Good Earth: A Celebration of Growing Food Around the World*. New York: Harry N. Abrams, 1993.

Anderson, Edgar. *Landscape Papers*. Berkeley: Turtle Island Foundation, 1976.

Arnold, Steven F., et al. "Synergistic Activation of Estrogen Receptor with Combinations of Environmental Chemicals." *Science*, June 7, 1996: 1489–92.

Benbrook, Charles M. *Pest Management at the Crossroads*. Yonkers, N.Y.: Consumers Union, 1996.

Berry, Wendell. *The Unsettling of America: Culture and Agriculture*. San Francisco: Sierra Club Books, 1977.

Bourn, Diane M. "The Nutritional Value of Organically and Conventionally Grown Food — Is There a Difference?" *Proceedings of the Nutrition Society of New Zealand* 19 (1994): 51–57.

Bradley, Fern Marshall, and Barbara W. Ellis, eds. *Rodale's All-New Encyclopedia of Organic Gardening: The Indispensable Resource for Every Gardener*. Emmaus, Pa.: Rodale Press, 1992.

Buchmann, Stephen L., and Gary Paul Nabhan. *The Forgotten Pollinators*. Washington, D.C.: Island Press/Shearwater Books, 1996.

Caddick, Jim. "A Question of Taste." *Exploratorium Quarterly*, Winter 1990: 8–13.

Carson, Rachel. *Silent Spring*. Boston: Houghton Mifflin, 1962.

Cocannouer, Joseph A. *Weeds: Guardians of the Soil*. New York: Devin-Adair, 1950.

Cohen, Brian A., and Richard Wiles. *Tough to Swallow: How Pesticide Companies Profit from Poisoning America's Tap Water*. Washington, D.C.: Environmental Working Group Report, 1997.

Cohen, Brian, et al. *Weed Killers by the Glass*. Washington, D.C.: Environmental Working Group Report, 1995.

Colborn, Theo, et al. "Developmental Effects of Endocrine-Disrupting Chemicals in Wildlife and Humans." *Environmental Health Perspectives*, Oct. 1993: 378–84.

Davis, Devra Lee, and H. Leon Bradlow. "Can Environmental Estrogens Cause Breast Cancer?" *Scientific American*, Oct. 1995: 166–72.

Di Silvestro, Roger. "What's Killing the Swainson's Hawk?" *International Wildlife*, May/June 1996: 39–43.

Food Quality Protection Act of 1996, Public Law 104–170.

Garry, Vincent F., et al. "Pesticide Appliers, Biocides, and Birth Defects in Rural Minnesota." *Environmental Health Perspectives*, Apr. 1996: 394–99.

Gilbert, Susan. "America Tackles the Pesticide Crisis." *New York Times Magazine*, Oct. 8, 1989: 22–57.

Gillespie, Janet. *Peacock Manure and Marigolds: A "No-Poison" Guide to a Beautiful Garden*. New York: Viking Press, 1964.

Goldman, Lynn R., et al. "Pesticide Food Poisoning from Contaminated Watermelons in California, 1985." *Archives of Environmental Health*, July/Aug. 1990: 229–36.

Hart, Rhonda Massingham. *Using Beneficial Insects: Garden Soil Builders, Pollinators, and Predators*. Pownal, Vt.: Storey Communications, 1991.

Heavy Methyl Bromide Use near California Schools. Washington, D.C.: Environmental Working Group Report, 1996.

Hornick, Sharon B. "Factors Affecting the Nutritional Quality of Crops." *American Journal of Alternative Agriculture* 7 (1992): 63–67.

"India's Chemical Tragedy: Death Toll at Bhopal Still Rising." *Chemical and Engineering News*, Dec. 10, 1984: 6–7.

Klinkenborg, Verlyn. "A Farming Revolution." *National Geographic*, Dec. 1995: 60–89.

Maine Organic Farmer and Gardener. Sept./Nov. 1995–Sept./Nov. 1998.

Martin, Deborah L., and Grace Gershuny, eds. *The Rodale Book of Composting*. Emmaus, Pa.: Rodale Press, 1992.

Mitchell, John G. "Our Polluted Runoff." *National Geographic*, Feb. 1996: 106–25.

Moses, Marion. "Pesticide-Related Health Problems and Farmworkers." *Official Journal of the American Association of Occupational Health Nurses*, Mar. 1989: 115–30.

Murphy, Pat. "The Glorious Potato." *Exploratorium Quarterly*. Winter 1990: 20-24.

National Research Council. *Pesticides in the Diets of Infants and Children*. Washington, D.C.: National Academy Press, 1993.

Nebel, Bernard J., and Richard T. Wright. *Environmental Science: The Way the World Works*. Englewood Cliffs, N.J.: Prentice-Hall, 1993.

Perkins, John H. *Insects, Experts, and the Insecticide Crisis: The Quest for New Pest Management Strategies*. New York: Plenum Press, 1982.

Pimentel, David, and Hugh Lehman, eds. *The Pesticide Question: Environment, Economics, and Ethics*. New York: Routledge, Chapman and Hall, 1993.

Pleasant, Barbara. *The Gardener's Bug Book: Earth-Safe Insect Control*. Pownal, Vt.: Storey Communications, 1994.

Rhoades, Robert E. "The World's Food Supply at Risk." *National Geographic*, Apr. 1991: 75–105.

Riotte, Louise. *Carrots Love Tomatoes: Secrets of Companion Planting for Successful Gardening*. Pownal, Vt.: Storey Communications, 1975.

Roderick, Kevin. "Cancer Cluster Claimed in Farm Town of Earlimart." *Los Angeles Times*, Sept. 15, 1989.

Rowell, Galen. "Falcon Rescue." *National Geographic*, Apr. 1991: 106–15.

Schrader, Esther. "A Giant Spraying Sound." *Mother Jones*. Jan./Feb. 1995: 34–73.

Soto, Ana M., et al. "The Pesticides Endosulfan, Toxaphene, and Dieldrin Have Estrogenic Effects on Human Estrogen-Sensitive Cells." *Environmental Health Perspectives*, Apr. 1994: 380–83.

Stinson, John C., et al. "Pesticide-Contaminated Cucumber" (letter). *The Lancet*, Jan. 2, 1993: 64.

U.S. Department of Agriculture, Agricultural Marketing Service. *Pesticide Data Program Annual Summary, Calendar Years 1993–96*. Washington, D.C.: USDA.

U.S. Department of Agriculture, National Agricultural Statistics Service. *Washington Fruit Chemical Usage Survey, Apples, 1995 Crop*. Washington, D.C.: USDA.

U.S. Environmental Protection Agency, Office of Atmospheric Programs, Division of Stratospheric Protection, Methyl Bromide Program. *Methyl Bromide Phase-Out Web Site*. Washington, D.C. www.epa.gov/spdpublc/mbr/mbrqa.html

Ware, George W. *Pesticides: Theory and Application*. New York: W. H. Freeman, 1983.

Wargo, John. *Our Children's Toxic Legacy: How Science and Law Fail to Protect Us from Pesticides*. New Haven: Yale University Press, 1996.

Wheelwright, Jeff. "The Berry and the Poison." *Smithsonian*, Dec. 1996: 41–50.

Whorton, James. *Before Silent Spring: Pesticides and Public Health in Pre-DDT America*. Princeton, N.J.: Princeton University Press, 1974.

Wiles, Richard, et al. *A Shopper's Guide to Pesticides in Produce*. Washington, D.C.: Environmental Working Group Report, 1995.

———. *Overexposed: Organophosphate Insecticides in Children's Food*. Washington, D.C.: Environmental Working Group Report, 1998.

Wilk, Valerie A. "Health Hazards to Children in Agriculture." *American Journal of Industrial Medicine* 24 (1993): 283–90.

Winston, Mark L. *Nature Wars: People versus Pests*. Cambridge, Mass.: Harvard University Press, 1997.

Wynne, Peter. *Apples: History, Folklore, Horticulture, and Gastronomy*. New York: Hawthorn Books, 1975.

Environmental Working Group web site: www.ewg.org

Index

Page numbers in italics refer to photos.